8/11

MONSTER MANIA

VAMPIRES

John Malam

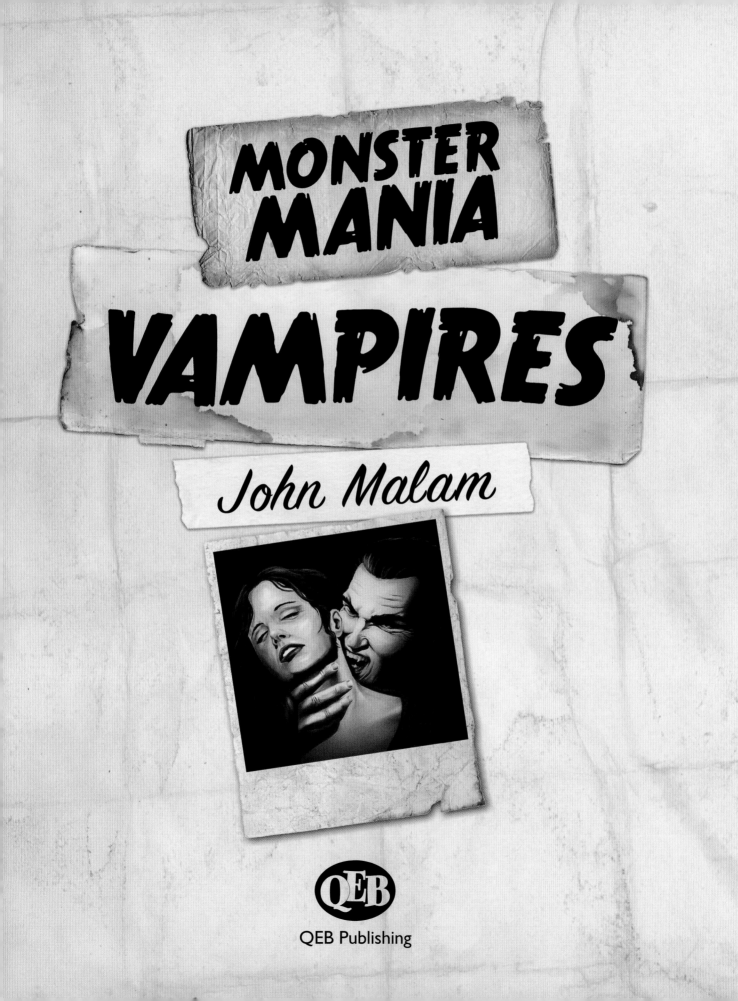

QEB

QEB Publishing

~m~

Illustrator: Vincent Boulanger
Editor: Amanda Askew
Designer: Matthew Kelly
Picture Researcher: Maria Joannou

Copyright © QEB Publishing, Inc. 2010

Published in the United States by
QEB Publishing, Inc.
3 Wrigley, Suite A
Irvine, CA 92618

www.qed-publishing.co.uk

Library of Congress Cataloging-in-Publication Data

Malam, John, 1957-
Vampires / John Malam.
p. cm. -- (QEB Monster mania)
Includes bibliographical references and index.
ISBN 978-1-59566-749-6 (library binding : alk. paper)
1. Vampires--Juvenile literature. I. Title.
BF1556.M34 2011
398'.45--dc22

2010008528

Printed in China

Words in **bold** can be found in the Glossary on page 31.

Acknowledgments

Alamy Images Johner Images 20r, Photos 12/Archives du 7eme Art 21b, 25b, 30,
Mary Evans Picture Library 24; **Bridgeman Art Library** Kharbine-Tapabor, Paris,
France 25t; **Corbis** Bruno Ehrs 13r; **Istockphoto** FotografiaBasica 9b, Mediadeva
13l, René Mansi 20l, Ideeone 29b; **Photolibrary** Superstock 28; **Rex Features**
SNAP 4, 16; **Shutterstock** Gian Corrêa Saléro 1, 8, Stephen B. Goodwin 9t, Csaba
Peterdi 12, Craig Dingle 17b, Petr Pilar 21t, Nikola Bilic 29tl, Flashgun 29tr,
Hannah Eckman 29c (bullets), 29c (garlic) Dariusz Majgier; **Topham Picturepoint**
Fortean/Sibbick 5, The Granger Collection 17t

CONTENTS

A world of VAMPIRES

Who or what are vampires? From **folk stories** and accounts by investigators, it's clear that vampires are monstrous creatures—the **undead**.

Vampires have survived death, and have come back to prey on the living. They need food—blood. Sucking the blood of humans and animals, they leave their victims dead or barely alive.

Count Dracula is the world's most famous vampire. Here, he is played by Christopher Lee (Dracula, 1958) and is shown drinking the blood from one of his many victims.

The meaning of "vampire"

No one really knows where the word "vampire" comes from. Some people say it comes from the Lithuanian word wempti, which means "to drink." Some say it's from the Turkish word uber, meaning "witch."

Vampires are hunters of the night, and return to their resting places before the first light of day. They are feared by all, and hunted by a brave few who have done all they can to destroy them, before they can spread vampirism any farther.

4

WHO'S WHO AMONG VAMPIRES?

ANIMAL VAMPIRES

These supernatural creatures attack their prey and drink their blood. The chupacabra, or goat-sucker, of Puerto Rico and Mexico is a famous example.

Chupacabra comes from the Spanish words, *chupar*, meaning to suck, and *cabra*, meaning goat—together, they make goat-sucker. Eyewitnesses claim that many livestock, especially goats, have been attacked and their blood drained.

AND THE REST...

LIVING VAMPIRES

Real people who call themselves vampires, such as Countess Elizabeth Bathory (1560–1614), who bathed in blood.

SPIRIT VAMPIRES

Vampires that exist without physical bodies. They can float, fly, appear and disappear, and can change their shape at will.

UNDEAD VAMPIRES

Vampires that were humans. They were attacked by vampires, and have been transformed into undead creatures.

DRACULA, PRINCE OF DARKNESS

When Jonathan Harker, an English solicitor, reached the mountains of **Transylvania**, he entered Count Dracula's castle. Dracula planned to move to England, and Harker was there to help him.

As the days passed, Harker grew concerned about Dracula. Harker saw him only at night, and Dracula never ate or drank. When Harker discovered Dracula sleeping in a coffin in the daytime, he knew he was staring at a vampire.

This story comes from
ENGLAND and
TRANSYLVANIA

Dracula's daytime resting place was discovered by Jonathan Harker.

Leaving Harker prisoner in the castle, Dracula boarded a ship for England. In the daytime, he slept in a box filled with soil from his homeland, and at night he bit the sailors and drank their blood. As the ship approached England, it was wrecked in a storm. Dracula escaped.

Now in England, Dracula sucked the blood of a young girl, Lucy Westenra, who became very weak. When Abraham Van Helsing, a vampire hunter, examined her, he discovered that she had been bitten by a vampire. Nothing could be done to save her, and Lucy died.

Dracula, the Book

Dracula is the title of a book written by Irish author Bram Stoker (1847–1912). The book, published in 1897, has become the world's best-known vampire story.

The search was on to destroy Dracula, who had fled back to Transylvania. Vampire hunters, led by Van Helsing, opened the vampire's coffin and plunged a knife into Dracula's heart, and Jonathan Harker slit the monster's throat. Dracula was dead.

The ship that Dracula traveled to England on, the *Demeter*, ran aground off the coast of Whitby, northeast England.

How VAMPIRES are made

According to vampire stories, there are several ways in which a person becomes one of the undead. It is called **transformation**, or **turning**.

The best-known method is where the vampire bites its victim, usually on the neck, and drinks the blood. The vampire doesn't take too much blood, or the person will die. Instead, the person is left feeling very weak and under the vampire's control.

The vampire sinks its fangs into the victim's neck and drinks the victim's blood.

Power of the Moon

In folk stories, the Moon is often linked with strange events. If a person was born on the night of a new Moon, or as the Moon changed from a new to a full Moon, a person could change from human to vampire.

Long life

A person who became a vampire had cheated death. Instead of living for a short time, like a human, they could live for hundreds of years. They might even be immortal, which means they could live forever.

The vampire returns the next night, and drinks more of the victim's blood. Last of all, the vampire bites itself on the wrist. Blood pours from the bite, and the victim drinks it. As soon as the person tastes the blood, they are turned into a vampire and leave their human life behind.

For some vampires, their turning was the result of misfortune and bad luck. For example, eating meat from a sheep killed by a wolf was said to cause vampirism. If a cat jumped over a dead body, or if a shadow passed over it, it was thought the person would come back as a vampire.

People can be turned into vampires even after they have died.

Arnold Paole, VAMPIRE OF SERBIA

This is a true story from the 1720s, about Arnold Paole, who thought he had been attacked by a vampire.

After the attack, Paole searched for the vampire's grave, dug it up, and destroyed the creature. Then he smeared the vampire's blood on his body, and ate soil from its grave. This, he hoped, would save him from any more vampire attacks.

This story comes from
SERBIA

Arnold Paole dug up the vampire's grave to destroy it.

10

However, a few days later, Paole fell, broke his neck, and died. He was buried, but that wasn't the end of him. Rumors spread around the village that Paole had been seen, alive and well. Then, four villagers died, and people became convinced that Paole had come back as a vampire. His grave was opened...

Instead of finding a rotting body, Paole was well preserved. He seemed to have moved inside his coffin, and there was a trickle of blood from his mouth. Fearful, the villagers drove a stake through his heart, cut off his head, and burned his body to end the misery of his attacks.

Plague of vampires

Three years after Paole died, 17 villagers suddenly passed away. A girl said she had seen one of them alive some time later. These people had become bloodsuckers after eating meat from cattle said to have been bitten by Paole. Their graves were opened, a **stake** was driven through their hearts, and their bodies were burned.

By destroying Paole's body, villagers hoped to defeat the vampire he had become.

How to spot a VAMPIRE

Stories about blood-sucking vampires have been told for hundreds of years. They are full of clues to help people work out if there's a vampire nearby.

IN A CEMETERY

Cemeteries are often said to be the homes of vampires. They sleep under the ground in the day, and emerge at night to go about their thirsty work. Groaning sounds from graves, strange mists and fallen gravestones are signs that vampires might be nearby. Barking dogs in a graveyard and no birdsong are other warning signs of a vampire in the area.

Vampires are said to rest in peace in cemeteries, until darkness falls and they emerge from the ground.

THE VICTIMS

Maybe a person has been bitten, but hasn't drunk the vampire's blood yet. The obvious clue is a bite mark on the neck. Other symptoms are exhaustion, loss of appetite, and suddenly losing weight. Being scared of garlic can also show that the person might be under a vampire's control.

A bite from a vampire usually has two holes where the fangs break the skin.

Look into the eyes

Vampires have very distinctive eyes. The pupils are big and dark, just like the eyes of owls and other animals of the night. The whites are not white at all, but blood-shot red.

Red eyes, piercing fangs, pale skin—it has to be vampire.

VAMPIRE BEHAVIOUR

Vampires have fangs, stinking breath, long fingernails, a pale complexion, black blood, and hairy palms. They're never seen in the day, and will always avoid bright lights at night. They don't eat "normal" food, and have powerful senses of smell and hearing. Some vampires can **shape-shift**, transforming themselves into mists or animals, especially bats.

Mercy Brown, VAMPIRE CHILD

Mercy, her mother, and sister were all buried in the Rhode Island cemetery.

O f all the world's vampire stories, this one is one of the strangest. What you are about to read is absolutely true…

George and Mary Brown lived with their three children in a small town in Rhode Island. Mrs. Brown and her daughter, Olive, fell ill with tuberculosis, a lung disease. Nothing could be done and they died. Then another daughter, Mercy, caught the disease and passed away.

Mr. Brown now feared for Edwin, his son, who was becoming ill. Rumors spread that one of his dead sisters, or even his mother, was a vampire. There was only one way to save Edwin—they had to check the bodies for signs of vampirism.

When the lid on Mercy's coffin was lifted, her body was found to be in good condition. Stranger still, it looked like she had moved. A doctor removed her heart, and it was found to be full of blood. Mercy Brown was undead, a vampire!

Her heart was burned and its ashes were mixed with medicine and given to Edwin to drink. Mr. Brown hoped the awful medicine would save Edwin, but it didn't, and the boy died from his illness.

Healthy Heart

Digging up the body of a dead person was often the first step in detecting a vampire. If the heart was healthy and full of blood, it was taken as a sign that the dead person was one of the undead.

Mercy's heart seemed fresh and was full of blood, as if it was somehow still alive.

POWERS OF VAMPIRES

Storytellers have given incredible powers to vampires, which are more than enough to frighten humans.

The key power of a vampire is its ability to live off blood. A vampire isn't a fussy eater, and will drink both animal and human blood. It is much more than just food. Blood gives a vampire another of its abilities—the power to live for a long time, maybe even forever.

A vampire has power over life and death. If it takes too much blood, the victim dies. But, if it drinks just enough to leave the person helpless, the victim is one step closer to changing into a vampire.

Vampire stories and movies, such as Nosferatu, the Vampyre (1979), show how the bloodsuckers drink their victims' blood.

Vampires, unlike humans, have the power of flight, and they can cling onto walls and scramble up them, just like many of nature's flying creatures. Wherever they fly to, vampires spread disease.

Vampires have supernatural strength—perhaps they absorb this from their victims, so the more people they kill, the stronger they become. They have the power of mind control, and their human victims fall under their spell.

The Victorians imagined vampires as well-dressed, refined creatures.

Shape-shifters

Vampires can shape-shift at will, changing themselves into animals, especially bats, cats, wolves, dogs, rats, and fleas. They can also become mists and vapors, which allows them to enter victims' houses through gaps around doors and windows.

17

The shoemaker VAMPIRE

From Poland comes this sinister tale about a shoemaker transformed into a vampire. The citizens of Wroclau thought a vampire had descended upon them.

It all began on September 20, 1591. An unhappy shoemaker cut his own throat and died. His poor wife covered up the cut, so that no one would know he had taken his own life, and he was laid to rest in the local cemetery.

When people began to say they had seen the shoemaker's ghost, and it had pinched them as they slept, questions were asked. No one felt safe. Finally, the shoemaker's body was dug up.

The townsfolk were afraid to sleep at night, fearing the vampire would pay them a visit.

Are vampires real or not?

In the 1600s and 1700s, there were so many reports of vampires in eastern Europe that the Christian Church decided to investigate. A monk, Dom Augustin Calmet, studied the reports and decided that only superstitious people believed in vampires.

Executed criminals, as well as people thought to be vampires, were buried in unholy ground outside the town.

This story comes from
POLAND

The body was in good condition and hadn't rotted away—a clear sign of vampirism. It was reburied by the town gallows, in **unhallowed** ground. The sightings continued, so the vampire was dug up for a second time, chopped to pieces, and burned until all that was left was ash. The vampire was finally destroyed.

19

Protection from VAMPIRES

There was once a strong belief in vampires, especially in Europe. Many people were so scared by the thought of these vile creatures, they went to great lengths to protect themselves.

A home could be protected by planting thorn bushes around it, such as holly, hawthorn and wild roses. Their branches were cut off and put against doors and windows, creating a thorny barrier.

Vampires were thought to be fascinated by knots. Some people protected their homes with fishing nets draped in the windows—a vampire would leave them alone because it would have to undo all the knots.

Thorny bushes, especially roses and hawthorn, were thought to provide a magical defence against vampires.

Vampires not welcome

A vampire can enter a house only if it's invited to step inside. However, if the person doesn't know the visitor is a vampire, then it's easy for the monster to trick its way inside.

Garlic was thought to offer protection from vampires, who hate its smell. Crushed garlic was smeared around doors and windows. Garlic bulbs were strung up around the house, worn as necklaces, or just tucked into a pocket.

Strings of garlic bulbs were placed around the house, indoors and outdoors, because vampires dislike the strong smell.

Seed power

One trick was to spread thousands of seeds or handfuls of sand onto the floor. Vampires were obsessed with counting, so they would stop to count the masses of tiny specks. They would still be counting as the sun started to rise, at which point they would retreat to their lair.

Vampires have strong senses. Bright candles were kept burning in homes to keep vampires away. The sound of ringing bells offered protection as vampires hated the noise. They also had a fear of crosses, which were painted on doors with tar. Its strong smell kept vampires well away.

A hunter holds up a cross to Count Dracula (played here by Christopher Lee in Dracula, 1958). Vampires fear the cross.

El Chupacabra
VAMPIRE
GOAT-KILLER

The first eyewitness reports of strange creatures were made in the 1540s, when hundreds of animals were drained of blood.

A group of Spaniards was moving a herd of cattle. They set camp for the night, and overnight, 1,500 cattle were killed.

About 400 years later, farmers on the island of Puerto Rico spoke about a creature they called El Chupacabra, which means "the goat-sucker."

In the still of the night, a mysterious blood-sucking creature destroyed hundreds of cattle.

The creature was biting their animals, especially goats, and drinking their blood. The creature was covered in fur, with batlike wings, staring red eyes, and a row of spikes along its spine. It could run, jump, and fly at great speed.

Animal vampires

Many stories exist of animal vampires, particularly dogs. Vampire dogs were blamed for attacks on livestock in Scotland, U.K., in the early 1800s, when sheep were found with bite marks to their neck.

Sightings of and attacks by El Chupacabra creatures are still being reported in Mexico, Chile, and the United States. Goats, horses, sheep, and dogs have all been found dead with bite marks.

Based on eyewitness reports, this is what El Chupacabra might look like.

Looking for VAMPIRES

In some parts of eastern Europe, people tracked vampires. They were known as **dhampirs**, half-human, half-vampire. They worked on the side of humans and they had the power to see vampires.

Dhampirs ripped the sleeves off shirts, and held them up like telescopes. This was how they could see a vampire that no one else could. Having spotted one of the undead, the vampire hunter would order the creature to leave—or kill it with a silver bullet.

The end of a German vampire, when a red-hot iron is plunged into his heart until all that is left is a skeleton.

To spot a vampire when it was sleeping in its hideaway, vampire hunters searched cemeteries. The hunter would pay particular attention to graves with fallen or sunken gravestones—signs that vampires might be under the ground.

If a grave was thought to contain a vampire, the body was dug up and examined by the vampire hunter for signs of vampirism, such as fresh skin, long nails, long hair, and fresh blood.

A gunshot with a silver bullet was thought to be one way to destroy a vampire.

Vampire hunter

The most famous vampire hunter was Professor Abraham Van Helsing, a doctor from Holland. He was a character created by Bram Stoker, the author of *Dracula*. In the book, Van Helsing leads the hunt for Count Dracula. The film *Van Helsing* (2004) stars Hugh Jackman as the monster hunter.

Peter Plogojowitz,
THE HUNGRY VAMPIRE

Eastern Europe seemed to be infected with vampires in the 1700s. There was one strange case—Peter Plogojowitz, an old farmer who became a deadly bloodsucker.

Peter died in 1725, in his village of Kisolava, Serbia. He was buried, but then his son claimed that his father was alive and well, and had come to him, demanding food. The son did as he was told. The next night, when Peter returned, his son refused to give him food. The son was found dead the following morning.

The son gave food to the vampire, but then, when he refused, the creature killed him.

Over the next few days, several villagers died in mysterious circumstances with blood taken from their bodies. Others said they had seen Peter, or dreamed that he had bitten them and sucked their blood.

Frightened villagers destroyed the vampire that had descended upon them.

Vampire madness

Stories of vampires were widespread in Germany, Austria, and Serbia in the early 1700s, leading to **vampire hysteria**. Churchyards were attacked and bodies dug up in a search for signs of the undead.

Panic set in. Soldiers were sent for, and Peter's grave was opened. Instead of finding his skeleton, they saw that his body was well preserved, and his mouth was stained with blood—clear signs of vampirism. A stake was driven through Peter's heart and his body was burned until all that was left was ash.

How to destroy a VAMPIRE

First find a vampire, then destroy it. The only way to defeat a bloodsucker is to destroy it as completely as possible, otherwise it will carry on infecting and killing its animal and human victims.

A vampire had to be staked to be destroyed. Stakes were made from branches cut from thorny trees, which were harmful to vampires.

The vampire was tracked down to its lair, and a long stake was hammered through its heart, and into the ground. This pinned the creature to the ground and stopped the flow of blood around its body. Vampire hunters took great care not to get splashed by the blood, as it drove people crazy.

The final moments for a sleeping vampire, about to be killed with a wooden stake plunged through its heart.

After the staking, the vampire's head was cut off, ideally with a gravedigger's spade. The mouth was stuffed with garlic and the head was boiled in vinegar. Then, the body was shot with a silver bullet, fired by a priest.

The headless body might be buried at a crossroads, and the head somewhere else. Crossroads were places of evil activity, where witches and vampires were buried. Or the vampire's head and body might be thrown onto a fire and burned to ash.

A vampire hunter's toolkit may contain a spade, vinegar, silver, and garlic. Silver was thought to be the purest of all metals, so it could defeat evil and kill vampires.

A vampire's body was buried in a separate place to the head to make sure that the vampire was completely destroyed.

Bottling a vampire

In Bulgaria, vampire hunters trapped their prey inside bottles. They forced the creature into hiding, where it stayed for days without food. The hunter put food inside a bottle to tempt the hungry vampire, and when it shrank itself down and flew into the bottle, the hunter quickly sealed it.

TIMELINE

1431–1476 Life of Vlad Dracula, known as Vlad Tepes (Vlad the Impaler). He impaled his enemies on wooden stakes.

1540s First reports of El Chupacabra in Arizona and New Mexico.

1720s The cases of Peter Plogojowitz and Arnold Paole, both from Serbia.

1734 The word "vampyre" came into the English language.

1810 Stories appeared in Scotland of sheep being drained of blood.

1819 The first vampire story written in English came out. It was by John Polidori and was called "The Vampyre."

1892 The case of Mercy Brown.

1897 The book *Dracula*, by Bram Stoker, was published.

1922 *Nosferatu*, a silent movie made in Germany, was released. It was based on Bram Stoker's book *Dracula*.

1976 Publication of the book *Interview with the Vampire*, the first of a series of vampire stories by Anne Rice. The movie of the book was released in 1994.

1997 The TV series *Buffy the Vampire Slayer* began, starring Sarah Michelle Geller.

2004 In Romania, a man suspected of being a vampire was dug from his grave and his heart was burned to ashes.

2005 In Birmingham, England, rumors spread about the "vampire of Alum Rock," which was reported to have bitten people at night.

2005 Stephanie Meyer's book *Twilight*, the first of a series of vampire stories, became a worldwide bestseller.

The second movie in the Twilight saga was released in 2009.

THE NEXT CHAPTER BEGINS

twilight
new moon

11.20.09

GLOSSARY

DHAMPIR

A hybrid creature thought to be part vampire, part human. Dhampirs, who came from eastern Europe, were good at detecting vampires.

FOLK STORIES

Traditional stories told in particular regions of the world. They began as spoken word stories, and may have been very old by the time they were written down for the first time.

SHAPE-SHIFT

The ability of a vampire to change its shape from one thing into another, such as a bat or a mist.

STAKE

A wooden stick with a pointed end, used to kill a vampire by stabbing it through its heart.

TRANSFORMATION

The process of changing a human into a vampire.

TRANSYLVANIA

A mountainous region of Romania, southeast Europe, which is the setting for Bram Stoker's vampire novel about Count Dracula.

TURNING

Another word for transformation. A person who became a vampire had been "turned" into one of the undead.

UNDEAD

A creature, such as a vampire, that lives in two worlds—the world of the living, and the world of the dead.

UNHALLOWED

Unholy ground that is linked with evil and harmful forces.

VAMPIRE HYSTERIA

When many people in a community panic because they think they are threatened by one or more vampires.

INDEX